DISCOVERING THE TECHNOLOGY OF
ANCIENT CHINA

LINDSEY LOWE

Cavendish
Square

Published in 2024 by Cavendish Square Publishing, LLC
2544 Clinton Street, Buffalo, NY 14224

Portions of this work were originally authored by Charlie Samuels and published as *Technology in Ancient China*. All new material this edition authored by Lindsey Lowe.

Website: cavendishsq.com

Children's Publisher: Anne O'Daly
Design Manager: Keith Davis
Designer: Lynne Lennon
Picture Manager: Sophie Mortimer

Picture Credits
Front Cover: iStock: pinggr b; Shutterstock: Izmael t.
iStock: blackred 40, Chalffy 43; Public Domain: 11, 21; Shutterstock: 17, 34, Antonio Abrignani 32, Venus Angel 5, Robert Anthony 27, Norman Chan 31, Hung Chung Chih, 37, jorisvo 28, William Ju 20, Kentoch 16, L.F 35, Valery Shanin 6, Yanfel Sun 10, P. Witthaya 42; Thinkstock: Hemera 38, Ingram Publishing 36, istockphoto 1, 9, 12, 13, 14, 15, 18, 22, 24, 33; Photos.com 8, 41; Top Photo Group, 4, 26.

Cataloging-in-Publication Data

Names: Lowe, Lindsey.
Title: Discovering the technology of ancient China / Lindsey Lowe.
Description: Buffalo, New York : Cavendish Square Publishing, 2024. | Series: Discovering ancient technology | Includes glossary and index.
Identifiers: ISBN 9781502669339 (pbk.) | ISBN 9781502669346 (library bound) | ISBN 9781502669353 (ebook)
Subjects: LCSH: Technology--China--History--Juvenile literature. | Science--China--History--Juvenile literature. | China--Civilization--Juvenile literature.
Classification: LCC T27.C5 L69 2024 | DDC 609.51--dc23

CPSIA compliance information: Batch #CSCSQ24: For further information contact Cavendish Square Publishing LLC at 1-877-980-4450.

Printed in the United States of America

Find us on

The Chinese gave the world papermaking, printing, gunpowder, the magnetic compass, the rudder, and a harness that transformed the use of horses. Many innovations were made by unknown artisans, while others were the result of technological breakthroughs by imperial officials.

LONG-LIVED CIVILIZATION

Chinese history is divided into dynasties from 3000 B.C.E. until the end of the imperial government in the early 20th century. The northern and southern parts of the country were originally separate, but were unified by the First Emperor, Qin Shi Huangdi, in 221 B.C.E. A long series of dynasties then rose and fell in China. Some of the most important were the Tang, Song, Yuan, Ming, and Qing dynasties. This book introduces the most important technological innovations behind this civilization.

China was so famous for its high-quality pottery and porcelain that the name "china" is used to describe all such objects.

TECHNICAL KNOW-HOW

Ancient China did not often come into contact with other cultures. The country was so vast and its civilization so advanced that it usually drew on technology from within China itself.

One of the earliest Chinese dynasties to develop a significant engineering technology was the Shang (c.1600–1045 B.C.E.). The Shang built vast tombs for their

The terracotta warriors of the First Emperor are evidence of the skills of early Chinese potters.

rulers. They dug burial chambers up to 40 feet (12 m) deep. Tomb engineering reached its peak with the magnificent tomb of the First Emperor, Qin Shi Huangdi (259–210 B.C.E.). He was buried in an underground re-creation of his capital city, complete with a river of mercury. He also ordered the construction of more than 8,000 life-sized pottery soldiers to protect him in the next life, together with horses and chariots. The warriors were made in molds but a layer of clay was added so that each warrior had a unique face.

METALWORKING

The ancient Chinese were also great metalworkers. The Shang used bronze to make weapons and vessels, but not tools. The tradition of metalworking continued. In the sixth century B.C.E., the Chinese were the first people to cast iron.

This bronze vessel was made in the fifth to third centuries B.C.E. Its decoration had religious meaning.

7

FARMING

The Chinese improved the plow. They also introduced the practice of growing rice in flooded fields.

The Chinese were 2,200 years ahead of Europe in farming technology. By the sixth century B.C.E. Chinese farmers were sowing their crops in neat rows while European farmers were still scattering seeds. Iron hoes helped Chinese farmers to weed the land, while the plow enabled them to loosen and turn the soil before planting.

The chief crops in northern China were wheat and millet, but in the warmer south the main crop was rice. From about 6500 B.C.E., the Chinese grew rice in waterlogged paddy fields. These were created on large, flat areas of land or on narrow terraces on steep mountainsides. By the first century B.C.E., farmers used a multi-tubed seed drill to speed up sowing in rows.

METAL EQUIPMENT

The iron plow first appeared in the sixth century B.C.E. It had a blade specially shaped to cut through the soil. The plow was pulled by oxen or water buffalo.

TECHNICAL SPECS

» In the sixth or fifth century B.C.E., the Chinese invented the cast-iron hoe, which made weeding easier.

» The development of the swan-neck hoe in the first century B.C.E. meant farmers could weed around plants without damaging them.

» In the first century B.C.E., the moldboard plow was invented. It turned the soil, releasing nutrients. It let farmers work less fertile soil.

» The square-pallet chain pump raised water through a series of wooden platforms (pallets) that were attached to a metal chain. One pump could raise water 12 feet (4 m).

Farmers began planting in rows in the first century B.C.E. It made crops easier to weed and harvest.

FLOOD CONTROL

The seasonal flooding of rivers spread nutrient-rich silt over the crops in the fields. However, rivers such as the Huang He (Yellow) and Chang Jiang (Yangtze) could be destructive. Too much flooding regularly ruined the crops and killed thousands of people. The Huang He River was known as "China's Sorrow."

China's rivers frequently overflowed their banks; this was both a blessing and a curse as the floods killed many people.

In the highlands, China's rivers run through gorges gathering sediment that is deposited downstream.

The Chinese tried to stop the rivers from overflowing their banks. They lined the water channels with reinforcements such as fascines or gabions to prevent erosion. Artificial earth banks called levees were also built along the rivers.

DIVERTING WATER

Around 256 B.C.E, an official named Li Bing built the Dujiangyan irrigation system on the Minjang River. Its purpose was to irrigate a large area of land and thereby prevent the city of Chengdu from flooding. The system diverted river water to irrigate the crops, drained sediment, and controlled the annual floods.

TECHNICAL SPECS

» Fascines and gabions were used to prevent erosion. Fascines are bundles of brushwood tied together; gabions are baskets or cages filled with stones.

» The Dujiangyan irrigation system is still in use today.

» A barrier divided the Minjang River into two streams, called the inner and outer rivers. A spillway diverted sand and stones from the inner river to the outer river. Like the neck of a bottle, the spillway took controlled amounts of water into the inner river.

» During the low-water season, 60 percent of the river's flow was diverted into the inner river for irrigation. In the flood season, the direction of the flow was reversed to stop flooding.

11

NUMBERS

Early peoples first developed a counting system that gave each number its own name and character. However, the system was difficult and relied on remembering many numbers. In the fourth century B.C.E. Chinese mathematicians came up with a new decimal system using the digits 1 to 9.

The abacus is still used in some Chinese stores. Skilled operators make calculations at lightning speeds.

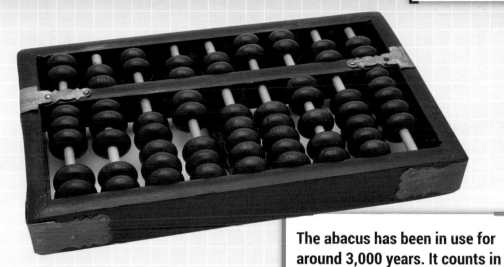

The abacus has been in use for around 3,000 years. It counts in ones, fives, and tens.

The Chinese system used the digits 1 to 9 and symbols for 10, 100, and 1,000. These few symbols could be combined to write any number.

RODS AND THE ABACUS

The Chinese invented the idea of zero. Mathematicians calculated with bars called counting rods. They left a space for a zero; later, they used a character. For sums involving larger numbers, people used the abacus. This is a wooden frame with columns of beads on rods. The invention became a vital tool, not just for mathematicians, but also for astronomers and merchants.

TECHNICAL SPECS

» The Chinese use of 0 to 9 is the foundation of our decimal (meaning 10) system.

» The Chinese began using the abacus between 1000 and 500 B.C.E.

» An abacus had two decks separated by a bar. Each bead on the lower deck equaled one unit; those on the upper deck equaled five units. To count, the beads were slid toward the central bar.

» By the second century B.C.E, the Chinese used negative numbers, 100 years before Europeans. They used black rods for negative numbers and red rods for positive numbers.

PRINTING

The Chinese invented paper and ink. They also invented stone and wooden printing blocks. In the eleventh century they created movable type, which meant books could be printed in large numbers so that more people could read them.

Ts'ai Lun, head of the imperial workshops, is said to have invented paper in C.E. 105. Early paper was made from rags, bamboo, mulberry bark, wheat stalks, and even rice. The fibers were separated, then soaked. A film of fibers was spread on a paper mold and left to dry. However, this paper was hard to write on, so people continued writing on pottery, silk, and even turtle shells.

In movable type, symbols were carved into individual blocks that could be put together as a page of text.

PROCESS OF PRINTING

Printing was a slow business. A whole page of characters was carved onto a stone block; ink was applied and then paper was pressed against the stone to make a printed page. By the eighth century C.E., printers used wooden blocks that were easier to carve. In 1041, Bi Sheng created movable type. Chinese characters were each carved into a separate block. They were then assembled to make a page, but could be reused to make another page.

In Chinese script, characters stand for words rather than letters; there are many thousands of characters.

TECHNICAL SPECS

» The first Chinese books were made from bamboo strips that were tied together.

» Tien Lcheu invented "Indian ink" in 2697 B.C.E. It was a mix of lamp oil, soot from smoke, gelatin from donkey skin, and musk from deer.

» The first books made from paper were rolled into long scrolls.

» The world's first printed book, the Diamond Sutra, was printed from woodblocks in C.E. 868.

» Blocks for movable type were carved in clay, which was then baked to make it hard.

» Wood blocks for up to 80,000 different characters were needed to print a book.

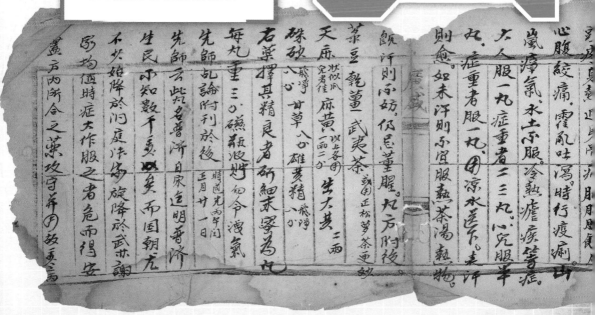

MONEY

Early civilizations did not use money. They used a system called bartering, where goods were swapped for other goods. It was the Chinese who first had the idea of money: a unit of value that could be exchanged for any type of goods. Money made trading easy and enabled people to move their wealth from one place to another.

Chinese money existed in various shapes for centuries before it became standard for coins to be round.

Coins were cast with characters explaining their origin. This proved that they were official currency.

Metal coins first appeared during the Zhou Dynasty (1046–256 B.C.E.). They were shaped as spades, knives, or shoes. These coins were heavy to carry. Later coins had a hole in the center to make them lighter. They were threaded on a string or belt and worn around the waist.

BANKNOTES

After the invention of paper and printing, paper money was introduced because it was easier to carry. Banks issued notes that could be exchanged for coins to the same value at another bank. By the Song Dynasty (C.E. 960–1279) everyone used this type of paper money.

TECHNICAL SPECS

» The earliest money in China appeared during the Shang Dynasty (1600–1045 B.C.E.), when people traded using cowrie shells.

» The First Emperor Qin (259–210 B.C.E.) standardized money throughout the country.

» The First Emperor introduced round bronze coins, called cash. They were in use for 2,000 years.

» Paper money was called flying money because it often blew away.

» Coins were made from silver until the First Emperor introduced bronze coins.

» Coins were cast in molds rather than being stamped, as in Europe.

BRONZE AND CAST IRON

China was transformed by the discovery of bronze and the invention of kilns. As early as 4000 B.C.E. the Chinese learned to make bronze by mixing copper and tin. Kilns heated metal ores to a high temperature. Metal replaced wood and pottery. It was used to make farming tools, containers, decorative objects, and weapons.

Chinese potters developed the first kilns as ovens to fire pottery, and later to melt copper. They worked out that adding tin lowered the melting point of copper, so the kilns did not have to be so hot. This made bronze, which had several advantages over copper.

This bronze vessel was an incense burner. The metal was colored by a process known as lacquering.

HOW TO...

Chinese craftsmen cast molten bronze in molds to make complicated shapes. The mold was made from clay. This one, right, used 10 pieces. There was a central core and an outer case with a lid and a base. The bronze was poured in through a hole at the top and filled the space between the core and the case. When it was cool, it was taken out and the mold was reused.

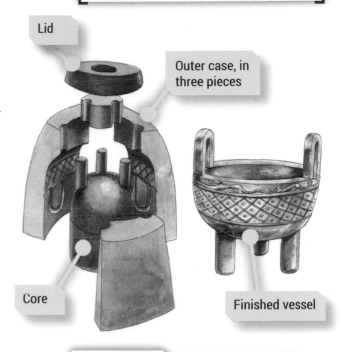

Lid

Outer case, in three pieces

Core

Finished vessel

Bronze was harder, so it lasted longer. Workers could cast bronze using molds. This allowed for the creation of complex objects.

IRON MAKING

From about 2000 B.C.E., the Chinese used blast furnaces to extract iron. A bellows blew a stream of air into the furnace to prevent the temperature from falling. Adding phosphorus to the iron lowered its melting point and the resulting hot liquid could be poured into a mold to cool. Europeans did not learn to cast iron until the Middle Ages.

TECHNICAL SPECS

» Changing the proportions of tin to copper created bronze in different colors and hardness.

» Iron was used in ancient China for farming tools, cast-iron pots and pans, and even toys.

» Blast furnaces existed in China almost 2,000 years before the process was discovered in Europe.

» By the fifth century B.C.E., good quality cast-iron farm tools and weapons were being produced.

» The Chinese made steel. Emperor Liu Bang (256–195 B.C.E.) was said to have a steel sword.

ASTRONOMY

The rulers of ancient China believed that their power to rule on Earth came from the heavens. The movement of planets and stars shaped their religion and politics. To keep the world in order, the emperor had to perform rituals according to an accurate calendar. Astronomers carefully watched the skies to calculate the passage of time.

In 52 B.C.E., the Chinese invented an armillary sphere. It used a series of interlocked rings to measure the paths of planets and stars. In C.E. 175 the design was improved to show the paths of the moon, planets, and sun. Astronomers could now accurately chart the sky.

This armillary sphere was made in the 17th century for the Chinese emperor.

The Chinese were among the first people to produce maps of the stars and to keep records of other things they saw in the skies.

The Chinese were among the earliest people to record the stars. They also noted events such as sunspots and supernovas. In 2005, archaeologists found the remains of one of the world's oldest observatories at Linfen in Shanxi province. It dates back 4,100 years.

MEASURING TIME

In addition to astronomy, the Chinese used water clocks to measure time. The simplest used water dripping through a hole to measure the passing of time. But water clocks could also be more complicated. Su Song (1020–1101) designed an astronomical clock tower. Powered by a waterwheel, the tower was 30 feet (9 m) tall.

TECHNICAL SPECS

» The calendar was based on the moon. A year had 12 months of 29 or 30 days, starting with the new moon.

» The Chinese use a cycle of 12 animals for the years. For example, 2023 was the year of the rabbit.

» The oldest Chinese mathematical text, from before 200 B.C.E., had many astronomical calculations.

» The Chinese observed sunspots as early as the fourth century B.C.E.; sunspots are cooler areas on the surface of the sun.

» An 11th-century C.E. water-driven astronomical clock mapped the stars as well as telling the time.

BUILDING CITIES

The buildings of Beijing's Forbidden City were laid out according to the rules of symmetry and feng shui.

From the Shang Dynasty (c.1600–1045 B.C.E.) onward, the Chinese people started to live in cities. These were built as a way to ensure social order and political control across the vast country. Cities were built with walls around them to protect them from outside invaders. Buildings were constructed from earth, timber, bricks, and tiles.

Cities and homes were built upon the same strict patterns. These were based on the rules of symmetry. Homes lined up on a north–south axis. They were built according to the rules of feng shui, which aims to harmonize the home by clearing the paths of invisible energy forces all around us.

CONSTRUCTION TECHNIQUES

Houses were built from earth packed inside a wooden frame. Once the wall was complete, the wooden frame was removed. Earth bricks were also used. In a palace, the bricks might weigh up to 110 pounds (50 kg). Roofs were made from earthenware tiles resting on a wooden frame.

PAGODA

Eaves

Square stories

Temple

TECHNICAL SPECS

» Feng Shui means "wind and water." It is based on the belief that everything is connected by an invisible force (qi), which must be allowed to flow at all times.

» Chinese Buddhists built pagodas. These towers were based on the shape of monuments in India, the homeland of Buddhism.

» Chinese pagodas had many stories, each marked by roof eaves. A wooden pagoda built soon after C.E. 600 at Chang'an was 330 feet (100 m) tall.

» The Forbidden City in Beijing was begun in 1406; the city within a city had more than 800 buildings for the imperial government.

THE GREAT WALL

The Great Wall of China is one of the largest human-made constructions in the world. It was built to protect China from attack by enemies in the north. The first sections date from the seventh century B.C.E. In 215 B.C.E. the First Emperor had the sections joined together. The most well-preserved section is 5,500 miles (8,850 km) long.

The Great Wall followed the shape of the landscape. Watchtowers were built at regular intervals to house soldiers on guard.

CONSTRUCTION

The earliest sections were made from compacted earth or from mud bricks: brick-making kilns were built at regular intervals along the wall. There were watchtowers along the whole length of the wall.

Watchtower

Wall follows contours of ground

Layers, or courses, of clay bricks

The earliest sections of the wall were built from compacted earth mixed with stones and twigs. Later, mud bricks were used. Brick-making workshops were set up all along the wall.

LATER ADDITIONS

During the Ming dynasty (1368–1644), the Wall was rebuilt in stone. Square towers were built at regular intervals along the wall to house soldiers. They signaled from one tower to another using flags, fires, and drums. A 12-foot (4 m) wide walkway ran along the top of the wall for marching soldiers. The total length of all sections of the Wall ever built was over 13,000 miles (21 km).

TECHNICAL SPECS

» The bottom of the wall was about 21 feet 4 inches (6.5 m) wide; the top was 19 feet (5.8 m) wide, and carried a 12-foot (4 m) walkway.

» The average height of the wall was 23 to 26 feet (7 to 8 m).

» Gateways jutted out from the wall at important intersections on trade routes. These fortified, 30-foot (10 m) tall gateways allowed people to pass through the wall. To keep them secure, they had double wooden doors with heavy metal bolts.

» The original workforce on the wall were criminals and farmers. Conditions were harsh. It was said that a worker died for every 5 feet (1.5 m) of completed wall.

TRANSPORTATION

China's paved roads were all built to a standard width to make it easier for vehicles to travel around.

The First Emperor (221–210 B.C.E.) connected the vast empire with roads and canals. The capital city, Xianyang, was connected to the furthest parts of the empire by a 4,350-mile (6,960 km) road. By the end of the second century B.C.E., China had 22,000 miles (35,200 km) of roads.

People traveled on foot, on horseback, or in horse-drawn carts and carriages. All roads were the same width and all carts were the same size, so they could travel on any road. The roads were paved with stone and lined with trees.

HORSE POWER

The invention of the horse harness in the fifth century B.C.E. changed the nature of transportation. The harness allowed horses to pull much heavier loads. Cloth stirrups were probably used by nomads such as the Mongols, but the biggest innovation for riders was the metal stirrup. The Chinese invented iron and bronze stirrups in the third century C.E.

TECHNICAL SPECS

» Chinese carts had two large wheels and silk covers to keep off the sun or the rain.

» The breastcollar harness invented by the second century B.C.E. allowed horses to use all their strength for pulling. It appeared in Europe over 1,000 years later.

» Stirrups gave riders stability, so they could ride for longer and further.

» Chinese travelers used maps to find their way around.

» Chinese maps put south at the top and north at the bottom.

» Chinese maps were the first to use grids and coordinates.

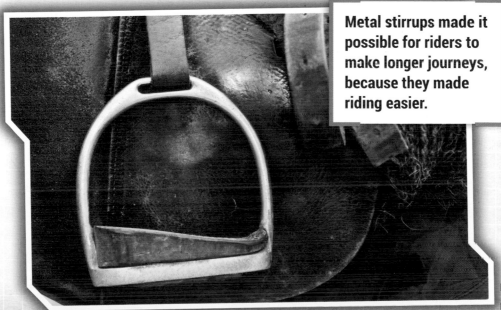

Metal stirrups made it possible for riders to make longer journeys, because they made riding easier.

GRAND CANAL

The great rivers of China, such as the Huang He (Yellow) and Chang Jiang (Yangtze), run mainly from west to east. The ancient Chinese built waterways that made it possible to travel virtually everywhere by boat. This was safer and faster than road transport, and was also the best way to carry goods such as grain.

The Grand Canal and its linked waterways joined a huge region of China together for the first time.

As early as the eighth century B.C.E., the Chinese had built waterways for irrigation. The first transportation canal was dug in the sixth or fifth century B.C.E. It connected the Huang He and Huai rivers.

GRAND CANAL

The Grand Canal was completed in the seventh century C.E. It was really a series of waterways that linked six river systems. It made it possible to travel by water from Hangzhou in the south to Beijing in the north. The canal is still in use today.

TECHNICAL SPECS

» The Grand Canal was the longest water system of the ancient world: 1,100 miles (1,760 km).

» As many as five million laborers worked on the construction of the Grand Canal.

» In C.E. 984 Assistant Transport Commissioner Qiao Weiyo invented the pound lock. This allowed barges to climb or descend in elevation with ease.

» In the mid-15th century, the government used 11,775 barges to move grain along the Grand Canal to China's cities; more than 121,500 soldiers worked on the grain boats.

HOW TO...

The pound lock had two sets of gates that shut with the boat between them. Sluice gates could then be opened in the upper or lower gate to allow the water level inside the lock to be raised or lowered. The next gate was then opened so that the boat could continue along the canal. Before the lock was invented, boats had to be raised or lowered between canals using ropes, which took a long time and was very dangerous.

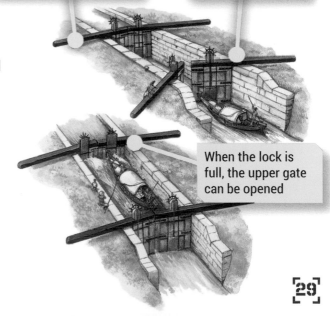

When the lower gate is closed, sluices are opened in the upper gate

The lower gate is opened so a boat can enter

When the lock is full, the upper gate can be opened

MARITIME TECHNOLOGY

The Chinese began to build new types of ships, such as the junk, during the Han Dynasty (206 B.C.E.– C.E. 220). Rudders and bulkheads appeared during the Song Dynasty (C.E. 960–1279), and China was the first civilization to develop the magnetic compass.

Chinese scientists learned about the magnetism of the Earth in about 2000 B.C.E. They also knew that a magnetic stone always turned north–south. They used such stones, called lodestones, to plot a ship's course or to steer in the dark.

THE JUNK

Junks are large ships with flat bottoms and raised sterns (backs), which make them stable and good for carrying cargo.

This model shows a Chinese compass with a magnetized spoon. The spoon's handle always pointed to the south.

The junk is in daily use in China. This is a tourist vessel, but junks are still used for transporting cargo.

SEAWORTHY

The junk's square sails were made from matting and divided into sections by wooden poles, known as battens. This allowed the sails to be partly raised or lowered. The rudder at the stern of the ship steered it by changing the flow of water past the hull. Bulkheads were small, watertight compartments in the junk's hull. They prevented it from sinking if it became holed. Such technological advances made the junk and other vessels reliable in open seas.

TECHNICAL SPECS

» The Chinese made the first compass with dials and pointers by rubbing a metal needle on a lodestone to make it magnetic.

» The rudder dates from the second century C.E. Previously sailors had used large oars to steer their ships. The rudder meant ships could be far larger. China's navy became the biggest in the world.

» Junk sails were made from natural fibers such as grass or bamboo.

» The Chinese invented paddleboats in the fifth century C.E. These were powered by men on treadmills turning waterwheels on the sides of the vessel.

FAMILIAR INVENTIONS

Many Chinese inventions are still used in everyday life. The original designs have never needed further improvement. They include the wheelbarrow, the umbrella, and the kite. Equipment for sports such as badminton also emerged in ancient China.

The wheelbarrow could carry heavy loads. The long handles acted as levers and made the barrow easier to push.

The first umbrellas were parasols made from paper. They provided shade. The paper was later covered with wax or lacquer to waterproof it.

The umbrella was invented in China up to 4,000 years ago. The first parasols were used to keep off the sun, rather than the rain. It was only later that parasols were made waterproof.

THE WOODEN OX

It is not known when the wheelbarrow was invented, but it appears in tomb paintings from the first century C.E. The large handcart was nicknamed the "wooden ox." They were used to transport everything, including people. Some versions had a front wheel; others had a central wheel.

TECHNICAL SPECS

» Wax and lacquer were used to waterproof paper parasols.

» The collapsible umbrella was in use by C.E. 21.

» Central–wheel handcarts could carry up to six people. The longer the handles, the less the force needed to move the barrow. Some wheelbarrows were even fitted with sails.

» The first kites appeared some 2,800 years ago. They were bamboo frames covered with paper or silk.

» The earliest use of kites was military. Kites were used to distract the enemy, and to send messages over long distances.

MEDICINE

Traditional Chinese medicine is popular in many parts of the world. It is based on the use of herbs and minerals.

The ancient Chinese believed that everything in the world had two opposing qualities: the yin and yang. These words literally mean "the dark side" and "the sunny side" of a hill, and represent opposites such as heaven and Earth, or birth and death. A sickness in the body was a sign that the yin and yang were out of balance. Doctors used techniques such as acupuncture and herbal remedies to restore the balance.

MEDICAL PRACTICE

Acupuncture works on the principle that the life force is contained in 12 lines (meridians) that link parts of the body. If a person becomes sick, a meridian is blocked. A tiny needle is inserted into the skin to unblock the meridian. Herbal, mineral, and animal remedies are even older than the use of acupuncture. Remedies are often taken in tea. Every remedy is made up for the individual, so no two remedies are the same. Many remedies, such as taking wormwood for fevers, are still used today.

TECHNICAL SPECS

» Some Chinese remedies used body parts from animals. There is still an illegal market for body parts from endangered species, such as tigers and rhinos.

» Male doctors were not allowed to touch female patients. Dolls were used to explain diagnoses.

» Acupuncture first appeared around 2700 B.C.E.

» In the 16th century C.E., Doctor Li Shizhen listed 1,892 herbs and 11,000 prescriptions in a book titled *Bencao Gangmu*.

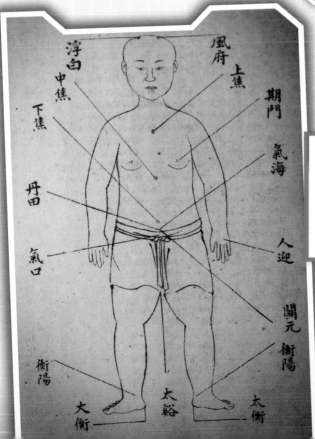

This early acupuncture diagram shows the needle insertion points used to cure a particular condition.

MAKING SILK

Silk was one of the greatest Chinese exports and the silk-making process was a closely guarded secret. Silk cloth was extremely valuable and only noble classes were allowed to wear it. Sometimes silk was used in place of money. Trading silk made China very wealthy. The routes from China to Europe were collectively known as the Silk Road.

Silk comes from the cocoon of the silk moth. The caterpillar spins a cocoon around its body while it changes into an adult. When the cocoon is put into boiling water the thread of the cocoon loosens. The long threads are then twisted together to make a strong yarn that can be used in weaving.

The fibers surrounding the cocoon of the silk moth can be pulled into a single thread several yards long.

TECHNICAL SPECS

» The silkworm increases almost 10,000 times in weight before it starts to spin its cocoon.

» A single silk moth lays between 200 and 300 eggs at a time, which hatch into silkworms.

» A cocoon can produce a thread up to 3,000 feet (915 m) long.

» It takes thousands of cocoons to make 3 feet (1 m) of cloth.

» Silk is so strong it was used to make the strings for ancient musical instruments.

» The Silk Road got its name because silk was the most valuable cargo to be traded from China to the West.

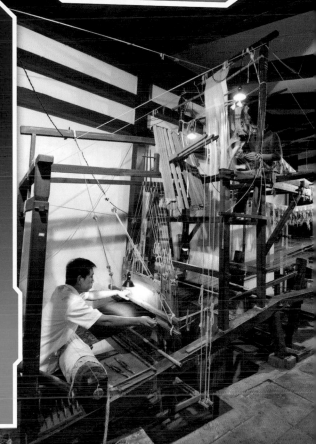

Silk is still woven by hand on looms similar to those used many centuries ago.

LONG HISTORY

Experts believe that the Chinese were weaving silk as early as 3000 B.C.E. The fabric has many advantages. It is light but strong, and is cool in the summer and warm in the winter. For centuries the cloth was so highly valued that only the emperor, his family, and the highest-ranking nobles were allowed to wear silk. Later the use of silk became more widespread. It was used for paintings, wall hangings, and decorations. Important documents were also written on silk.

WARFARE AND WEAPONS

Warfare in ancient China involved some of the most technologically advanced armies in the ancient world. The invention of the crossbow gave even unskilled archers the ability to kill people from long range. Although the ancient Chinese knew about gunpowder, they rarely used it for weapons.

For long periods of history, China was dominated by warlords who created their own private armies.

THE CROSSBOW

The crossbow was lightweight and accurate. It could only be developed thanks to advances in metal production. The bolt was released by a trigger pulled like that of a modern rifle.

Trigger for firing

Catch for holding taut string

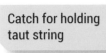

INTO BATTLE

China's warlords gathered armies of armored infantry, cavalry, charioteers, and crossbowmen. The first bladed weapons were made from bronze, which produced sharper blades than iron. The Chinese invented the crossbow before 450 B.C.E. to fire short, heavy arrows. The crossbow made chariots outdated, because archers did not need to get so close to the enemy. The infantry carried halberds. These shafted blades were fixed to the end of long bamboo poles, so they could be swung from a safe distance.

TECHNICAL SPECS

» Sun Tzu wrote *The Art of War* in the sixth century B.C.E. It was the world's first military handbook and its strategies are still used today.

» During the Battle of Changping in 260 B.C.E., more than half a million men were killed.

» Hand-to-hand combat was the most common type of fighting in Chinese battles. Most soldiers used axes or halberds.

» During the Shang dynasty (c.1600–1045 B.C.E.), armor was made from bamboo and wood and padded with cloth.

» The introduction of iron weapons from the sixth century B.C.E. meant that armor had to be tougher to resist penetration.

GUNPOWDER

The Chinese used gunpowder to make spectacular fireworks.

Gunpowder is thought to have been invented in China in the ninth century C.E. Some say that alchemists were trying to make a potion that would give them everlasting life. Instead, their mix of charcoal, sulfur, and saltpeter (potassium nitrate) caused an explosion. Gunpowder was used to make bombs, guns, rockets, and fireworks.

The gunpowder weapons invented by the Chinese in the 1280s became the basis of European cannons.

The first written reference to gunpowder was in 1044. The formula was called the "fire drug." The mixture burned and produced gases that expanded. If the gases were put in a sealed container, it exploded. If gunpowder was put in a tube that was open at one end, the hot gas shot out an iron ball. These weapons were the first firearms.

FIREWORKS

Gunpowder was later used to make fireworks. By adding different-colored chemicals to the mixture, the fireworks exploded into different colors.

TECHNICAL SPECS

» Fireworks were originally used to frighten off the enemy.

» Iron or steel dust was added to give fireworks a sparkling tail.

» Bombs filled with gunpowder were launched from catapults.

» Rockets were filled with gunpowder that was ignited to shoot arrows.

» In 1220 the Chinese made bombs with outer casings that shattered to produce shrapnel.

» The first gun dates from 1259, when pellets were fired from a bamboo tube.

» The Chinese gunpowder cannon dates from the 1280s.

PORCELAIN AND POTTERY

In China, pottery, or ceramics, is an art form as well as a way of creating useful objects. It has been produced in China for almost 15,000 years, and styles developed from simple, rough forms to complex, priceless porcelain pieces. Craftsmen developed innovative techniques for making and decorating ceramics. Porcelain production reached its peak during the Ming dynasty (1368–1644).

China has rich deposits of the clay and kaolin needed to make ceramics. With the necessary materials at hand, the Chinese took the raw products and made pots.

Chinese potters created sophisticated shapes. They were also famous for their complex decoration.

The potter's wheel was invented around 2000 B.C.E. This allowed potters to make perfectly round vessels with thinner walls. The vessels were fired in kilns. The Chinese introduced small vents in the kiln to keep the temperature constant during the firing process.

QUEEN OF CLAYS

Around the seventh century C.E., Chinese potters learned how to make porcelain. Porcelain is a mixture of kaolin and a mineral, feldspar. Unlike ordinary pottery, it is hard, very fine, and translucent. The Ming decorated their porcelain with blue and white patterns, and it became highly sought after in Europe.

TECHNICAL SPECS

» The earliest pots were hand built from coils of clay.

» Ordinary clay pottery is fired at temperatures between 930–2100°F (500–1150°C). Porcelain is fired at the much higher temperature of 2335°F (1280°C).

» When kaolin is fired at a high temperature, its physical makeup changes, a process known as vitrification. The kaolin becomes translucent and water resistant.

» At their peak, China's imperial potteries employed more than one million people and had 3,000 kilns.

Porcelain making is still a major industry in China; here a small bowl is painted by hand before being fired.

TIMELINE

B.C.E.

c.6500	Rice is domesticated in China.
c.5000	The Yangshao culture emerges in China.
c.5000	The first pottery is produced.
c.4000	The Chinese make bronze from copper and tin.
c.3300	The Liangzhu culture becomes prominent.
c.3000	The Longshan culture is the last of China's stone-age cultures to emerge.
c.2950	The Chinese develop a lunar calendar.
c.2700	Silkworms are cultured on mulberry leaves.
c.2700	Doctors begin using acupuncture.
c.2697	Indian ink is invented.
c.2296	Year 1 of the traditional Chinese calendar.
c.2000	Chinese astronomers record a first sighting of a comet.
c.2000	The potter's wheel is invented.
c.2000	The blast furnace is used to extract iron.
c.2000	The Xia culture becomes prominent at the start of China's bronze age.
c.1600	The Shang Dynasty rises to power on the north China plain.
c.1361	Chinese astronomers record a solar eclipse.
c.1360	Mathematicians begin using a positional number system.
c.1150	Chinese workmen cast bronze bells.
c.1100	The Chinese use spinning to make thread.
c.1046	The Zhou Dynasty replaces the Shang.
c.1000	Scribes begin writing on bamboo or paper.
c.900	The first cast metal coins are made.
c.700	The Chinese begin to cast iron.

c.600	Iron is used to make better plows.
c.600	The harness is introduced to make horses more useful for work.
c. 475	The Warring States period begins. It marks centuries of conflict between China's states.
c.400	The Chinese invent the crossbow.
c.400	The Chinese use counting rods for calculations.
C.221	Qin Shi Huangdi, the First Emperor, unifies China by defeating the individual kingdoms and founds the Qin Dynasty.
C.214	The main section of the Great Wall is completed.
C.210	Qin Shi Huangdi dies and is buried with a "terracotta army."
C.206	A revolt led by Liu Bang topples the Qin and begins the Han Dynasty. Han rule sees long-distance trade with Europe via the Silk Road.
C.105	Traditional date for the invention of paper in China.
C.100	Mathematicians begin using negative numbers.

C.E.

100	The multitube seed drill is introduced to plant seeds in rows.
100	The wheelbarrow appears.
220	The Three Kingdoms period begins as China fragments.
265	The rise of the Jin Dynasty restores order to China.
271	Invention of the magnetic compass.
302	Metal stirrups are in use by this time. The umbrella appears.
581	The short-lived Sui Dynasty begins its 40-year rule.
c.609	The Grand Canal is completed.
618	The Tang Dynasty begins a three-century rule.
c.725	Engineer Liang Ling-Zan constructs an astronomical water clock.

GLOSSARY

alchemist An early scientist who combined chemistry with magic.

Buddhism A religion that originated in India in the sixth century B.C.E.

canal An artificial waterway.

cast To pour molten metal into a mold and allow it to harden.

decimal A counting system that uses base 10.

dynasty A series of rulers from the same family.

empire A large territory ruled by an emperor or empress.

harness Straps used to control a horse or strap it to machines.

hoe A tool with a blade on a pole used for weeding crops.

irrigation Diverting water to the soil for agriculture.

kiln An oven used to harden pottery or bake bricks.

lodestone A type of magnetic stone.

moldboard plow A type of plow that turns the earth.

observatory A building used to observe the stars and planets.

pagoda A tower used as a temple or memorial.

parasol An umbrella used to provide shade.

porcelain A type of fine, translucent pottery fired at high temperatures.

seed drill A device that makes a hole in the soil to drop a seed into.

Silk Road A system of overland trade routes that stretched from East Asia through Central Asia to the Mediterranean.

spillway A place where water can overflow.

supernova The explosion of a very large star.

woodblock A way of printing in which a design is carved into a piece of wood.